UNKNOWN
SUPERSTAR

Books by Herbert Keyser

Women Under The Knife:
    A Gynecologist's Report On Hazardous Medicine

Prescription for Disaster:
    Health Care in America

Two Drifters Off To See The World

A Chautauquan Searches Paris For The Best Tarte au Citron

Geniuses of the American Musical Theatre:
    The Composers and Lyricists

An Unquiet Life:
    Odyssey of a Whistleblower (Fiction)

Finding Barbara:
    A Tale of Love, Greed, Misogyny and Genes

UNKNOWN
SUPERSTAR

Herbert Keyser

Published by Iridian Books
Los Angeles CA 90049

ISBN: 979-8-218-46900-9

Dedicated to the memory of
MORRIS AND DIANA KEYSER

INTRODUCTION

A year ago Walter Isaacson released his monumental book ELON MUSK. He describes Musk's behavior as being without even the most minimal level of empathy. It is the result, in Isaacson's explanation, of his Asperger's Disease. It is clear, in Isaacson's opinion, that this facet of Musk's personality is the force that has made him the great genius that he is. Musk's total disregard for those under him, and the resultant demands he makes of everyone he controls, by virtue of his wealth, have been nothing short of miraculous. One can speak negatively about his behavior. But not recognizing his genius, is foolhardy.

This book, however, is about another genius, one without wealth or stature. But, by contrast, he reached that goal while possessing great empathy and love for those in his private and public life. There is no one who did not have great love of his moral values and the treatment of all those around him, friends, coworkers and family.

Interestingly, these two men of such divergent personality traits, had many similarities. They each possessed a medical aspect to their lives that could be called a defect. In Musk's case, Isaacson demonstrates that the Asperger's was a significant strength.

In the case of our second genius, the affliction of deafness is present from the time of his birth. He never considered it a defect. In fact, it may have been the strength that resulted in his numerous accomplishments.

Another similarity in the lives of both of these men was the abusive behavior of their fathers. Isaacson considered that to be a part of Musk's driving force. Though the abuse of our second genius definitely was not well documented, it occurred more than one hundred years ago. It is difficult to know its importance, as there is no evidence of the effects on Morris. I never knew his father as I was born after his father's death.

Other characteristics were similar. Both men had an amazing work ethic. They were committed workaholics. Neither believed in ever taking vacations. They saw vacations as holding them back in their efforts. There was a significant difference still in the two of them. Our second genius believed in vacations for others around them, like family and employees. Unlike Musk, he possessed unlimited empathy for those around him. But Musk, because of the total absence of empathy believed that vacations were destructive to the work ethic of employees and discouraged them.

I believe that both of these men had a mindset that there was nothing they could not accomplish and strove for the ultimate level of success in their endeavors.

We all know a great deal about our first genius. I know much more about the second genius for a good reason. He was our father.

PROLOGUE

When my very special wife, Barbara, passed away after an unexplained brief illness, I had only one wish. It was to die as soon as possible. It was not a frivolous or illogical desire. She had not only been a spectacular wife. She had encompassed the entirety of what was special about my life. I did not take my own life then, however, because of the pleading of my wonderful son Christopher. However, it did not change my hope that my life would naturally come to an end soon. It was not a wish that was impossible or unrealistic as I was already in my late eighties.

Over the next several years I wrote the memoir about my wife, FINDING BARBARA. I then began having a slightly changed feeling about my own longevity. Starting about forty years ago, I cannot provide an exact date, I began researching and writing a biography of my father. That work sputtered along for years, constantly interrupted by other books and battles with the medical profession. Then it came to a sudden halt with the onset of Barbara's illness.

With only two people alive who have knowledge of our father's life, my brother, age 95 and me at age 91, I realized the selfishness of not dedicating myself to the completion of that book. The reason for the urgency, beyond our ages, is the simple fact that our father, Morris Keyser, was the greatest man I have ever known. His accomplishments were almost beyond belief. Beyond that, my knowledge that he was loved by so many people made it imperative that the story could not be allowed to vanish. The result is, I desperately now hope that I live long enough to complete the book and tell his story.

There are many individuals who are loved by family, friends and co-workers. In the case of Morris Keyser, I believe there was not one single person who knew him who did not have great love and admiration for him. It was impossible to do otherwise.

CHAPTER ONE

In 1888 Samuel and Anna Kaiser arrived in America. (Note the different spelling of their last name from Morris. There were many different spellings among all their children). I cannot be certain whether Samuel and Anna came to America together or separately. But, I am fairly certain they came separately. The documents indicate they had been residents of Minsk in Belarus. I know that Samuel (Our grandfather) was 32, born in 1856, when they arrived in America. Anna was two years younger. They were married in 1876 when Anna was 18 years of age.

In 1878 Anna had her first child Rebecca (called Beckie). There are no details about her birth, but the outcome indicates it was likely traumatic. She was deaf, blind and paralyzed, but I believe not mentally retarded for the remainder of her life. She lived in an institution for her entire life which went at least into her seventies. I saw her once when I was about ten years old. She was approximately 65 years old at the time.

Anna's next child Willie was born in 1880 and lived into adult life. Simon was born in 1882. The following year Fannie was born. Three years passed when she gave birth to Barney who was one of twins. His twin died at birth, not an uncommon occurrence in those years when the modern techniques of delivering twins was not yet fully understood. In 1888 she gave birth to Louis in Belarus.

Interestingly, Anna who was an Orthodox Jew, forbidden to use contraception, did not give birth again for six years. I have no information for certain when Anna came to America, but it is very possible she remained in Belarus when Samuel came in 1888, which would explain the long interval without children. In 1894 Gussie was born. Like Barney she was one of a set of twins in which her sibling died at birth.

In 1896 our father Morris was born. Anna was 38 years old by then. She had one more child, Harry. But I have no record of when he was born.

Rebecca was not the only one handicapped. It was a time when many children were born handicapped, many more than presently. One of the commonest of these handicaps may well have been deafness in a child whose mother contracted German Measles in the first trimester of her pregnancy. In our father's case another situation may have caused his deafness. It is known that women who have many pregnancies, going late into their fertile years, have a higher incidence of fetal problems in their later offsprings. Even though he was the eighth child who lived to adult life, there were many more pregnancies than that. Besides the demise of two twins, there may have been other children who died in early childhood, or many miscarriages as our father was the fifteenth of sixteen pregnancies. What makes late or defective eggs or sperm as a possible cause of his deafness is the fact that his brother Harry, born as the last child, was also deaf. Whatever the cause of our father's deafness, it had no other effect on the remainder of his faculties, as he was obviously the most brilliant of all his siblings.

On September 20th, 1896 Morris Keyser was born in a house at 7th and Rodman Street in Philadelphia. The home was called a bandbox house. They were also known as rowhouses. It was the cheapest way to build a home. Some row houses were more elaborate than others. Philadelphia was the first major city in America to utilize the concept. The city was laid out as a gridiron. Though originated in London, the design became prominent in Philadelphia around 1700. Constructed with wooden beams, the smallest had only one room on each floor. This is likely the size of the home in which Morris was born. The houses were 16 feet wide and 16 to 20 feet deep. There was a narrow spiral staircase and no indoor plumbing. Usually there were two or three stories. With such a large family, just imagining what life was like there is mind boggling. By the time they left Belarus, Anna already had four living children at home, Willie, Fannie, Simon and Barney. Beckie was not there as she had been institutionalized. But still to come were Gussie, Morris and Harry.

It has been impossible to find any information about what life was like there for them. But what is known was a complete disregard of Morris and Harry by their father and siblings. Interviews reveal an almost contempt for these two deaf children by all except their mother and brother Barney. They were seen as a burden by their father and siblings. These "burdensome" children did all the hard labor for the family. Anna was characterized as a loving mother, who saw Morris as a special child. She would be the first in a long line of individuals who, not only adored him, but saw great potential. Sadly, life for Harry was not the same.

Harry, born when Anna was about 40 years of age, had a problem beyond his absence of the ability to hear. Early on he began to have epileptic seizures which would haunt him all his life. As described by our father Morris, Harry was very strong and had the ability to do great things with his hands. Morris said aside from being able to repair anything, Harry created sculptures. But his illnesses became more and more debilitating, resulting in having him institutionalized in early adult life. The most information available indicated he died at age 44 during an epileptic seizure. Morris never talked much about his brother Harry. The obvious reason was that it depressed him. People who knew them said that any time a discussion came up about Harry, Morris would begin to cry.

When Morris was still a young child, one of his cousins reported to social workers that Morris was being mistreated. As a result, the social worker intervened and arranged for Morris to go to

Deaf School at the age of three. It was called the Belmont Avenue School, on Belmont and Monument Avenue. Miss Garrett was the principal. Two teachers took a very strong liking to Morris. They were Miss Zane and Miss Dalsemer. They would play a major role in his early development. All of this was at a much earlier time than his future wife, our mother Diana, attended the same school. Diana started when she was eight and a half years of age. The late start was not out of neglect. Her parents were dearly devoted to her and wanted Diana to remain at home rather than be sent to live away from home at a Deaf school.

When Morris was very young, he demonstrated to these teachers that he was not the run of the mill child. It was an interesting time in the development of deaf education. The staff of this school was becoming involved in a national disagreement concerning what was best for a deaf child. On one side of the debate was the judgement that deaf children suffered from a general belief, among the hearing public, that these children were not only deaf, but mentally retarded. All educators knew that was not true. But a contingent of them believed the deaf would be best served by trying to hide their deafness from the misinformed portions of the hearing public. Using sign language was a clear sign that they were deaf.

As a result, a philosophy developed that these children could be protected by not making their deafness obvious. This would be accomplished by avoiding sign language and learning to communicate by lip reading. Two of the most prominent individuals in that school of thought were Gov. Gifford Pinchot of Pennsylvania and Alexander Graham Bell. They both had deaf relatives. In Bell's case it was his wife. They devoted themselves to developing the philosophy that lip reading would be an advantage for them. Sadly, it was a terrible decision they had made which would become clear much later.

The obvious question might be, why would a person as brilliant as Bell seek such a different approach to the problems of the deaf. The answer becomes clear when one realizes that Bell's wife's deafness, which was the driving force for his efforts, did not originate at birth. She was born hearing and her deafness occurred later. Because she had heard, she spoke with no difficulty and only had to learn to lip read. The average deaf person did not have that advantage. They could not accomplish what Bell's wife had achieved and were unable to speak to most hearing people in a manner that made them readily understandable.

The result was a large portion of deaf children were discouraged from learning how to sign and spent their entire lives lip reading. The teachers at the school where Morris attended were strong supporters of Alexander Graham Bell's philosophy. and assisted in the powerful drive to end signing. What was so sad for me was the knowledge our father became a pawn as part of the driving force in this endeavor. It, of course, was not by his choice.

He was always an expert at lip reading. The leaders of the movement chose him as one of about a dozen students to be demonstration models of what could be accomplished without signing. He was only nine years old when they began parading this group of students in front of politicians, legislatures, business leaders, governors and even President Theodore Roosevelt. The physical proof I have about all of this is a silver ashtray. Engraved to him by President Theodore Roosevelt. A search through the White House records at the Library of Congress revealed a brief note about the meeting they had with the President. The promoters of this philosophy were a powerful group of leaders with contacts in the highest places. They did a terrible disservice to the advancement of deaf education. It was not done out of evil intent, just a total misunderstanding of what would best serve the deaf community. It took subsequent research to reveal that through the use of lip reading by the deaf, generally only about 50% of what was said was understood. But sign language was the equal of other language forms of communication.

Photos of Morris' father and mother posed by a professional photographer.

As a personal aspect of this, our parents for the remainder of their lives very rarely signed. It certainly had an effect on our mother. In our father's case, because of his brilliance, he was able to overcome it. However, their almost total lack of an adequate education would have a profound effect on their lives.

Photo of Morris' mother later in life, and allowed to smile

Photo of Morris and his mother in front of their South Philadelphia house. Morris is probably in his early twenties.

Photo of Morris' family on the farm. Morris is seen immediately to the right of the horse's head. He is probably in his late teens.

Photo of the silver ashtray, engraved to Morris Keyser, from President Theodore Roosevelt to Morris Keyser in 1906 when Morris was 9 years old. It is in the possession of his grandson, Christopher.)

Photo of Morris, probably at time of graduation from deaf school.

CHAPTER TWO

This story cannot be told or understood without an understanding of what it meant to be totally or profoundly deaf at the beginning of the 20th century. The general consensus of the hearing population was that the status of the deaf and the mentally retarded was essentially the same. The deaf population was a group that were a burden that needed to be cared for. No time should be wasted in bringing them into the society that functioned for the hearing. Their place in society was just to exist, and work and not to progress to any significant level. Education was just to the level to allow them to survive, but not to advance. The two main characters in this story, our parents, accepted this with indifference.

The main character, our father, though possessed of much more promising possibilities, was by far the more docile. Instead of resisting the mores surrounding the deaf, he did as he was told. The entire history of his life is described in his ability to never be confrontational. Through every bit of his history and every interview of his life, one thing was a constant. Every story described an individual who was kind, gentle and loving. He never showed anger. He never raised his voice. Every person in his family, his friends, his business associates, everyone saw him as being as close to being saintly as a human being could possibly be.

Our mother, as loving as my brother or I could possibly desire, was not that way in society. Unlike our father, in her entire life she never heard one single sound. But, that did not hold her back. Her parents adored her and did not want to send her to deaf school, but did so out of fear for her safety. They lived in the center of busy life in central Philadelphia. Diana, our mother cared nothing for the horse driven traffic and darted in and out of the street, in between carts and carriages and horses. Her parents, fearing she would be injured or killed accidentally, agreed by the time she was eight to send her to live at deaf school.

For the remainder of her life, she was always challenging what was expected for the deaf. As a late teenager, because she was considered a beauty in the deaf community, much to the disdain of her parents, she was dating the most popular deaf men. They were not necessarily of the highest social status. She would frequently date deaf prizefighters. Our grandparents would tell me later that she was not controllable by them, and they hated every deaf man they met that she was dating. Even with that "wild" period, it is worth noting here, when she at nineteen and our father at twenty-nine got married, they were both virginal.

Though her education was absolutely atrocious, and it would seem that she would be capable of doing nothing, she held down a position at a local department store with no difficulty. Though I have no evidence of what any testing would reveal about her, I have a belief, based on other information, that she must have been extremely bright and under-developed. Through the 49 years they were married Diana controlled everything in their lives other than Morris' professional life. She managed all their finances and other familial decisions that needed to be made. As in everything else, Morris concurred with every wish of hers, loved her dearly and demonstrated that in every way imaginable. The only thing that I believe he ever did that was against her wishes was smoke cigars. Even that, after a while, he gave up and stopped forever.

Diana, who loved to shop, would go by herself to the Department stores and buy things constantly. Because she was so frugal and they lived on the edge of poverty, the following day she would return everything. I think this was a game she played allowing herself to be an active member of the society of which she would like to be part. I often wondered, "Did the stores realize she was buying nothing?"

MY SWEETHEART

Morris and Diana early in their courtship. She was lucky to get him into a bathing suit. As the marriage progressed, he rarely went on vacation. He wrote "my sweetheart" on the picture he carried in his wallet.

Many many years later, when she was widowed and living alone in Philadelphia, an offer was made by the casinos in Atlantic City to seniors in Philadelphia in order to get them to come gamble in Atlantic City. The casino would provide free bus transportation to and from Philadelphia, a free box lunch and ten dollars worth of gambling chips to encourage them to gamble more. Our mother loved the opportunity. She would view it as a vacation and take the two hour ride to Atlantic City. She would sit on the boardwalk and have her lunch. Then she would walk for several hours on the boardwalk, window shopping, which she loved to do. Before leaving to return home she would go into the casino and cash in her ten dollars of chips and take the bus back. She had had a lovely day, a free lunch and earned ten dollars. That was our mother and everyone who knew her thought she was adorable.

CHAPTER THREE
MORRIS, DIANA AND THEIR CHILDREN

Education for the deaf today is eons ahead of what existed then. I do not recall ever having seen my mother read a book. Possibly as a child it was something she was encouraged to do in school. But, it was not continued in adult life. In my father's case I was told as a child he read prodigiously. He was recognized as an exceptional student at deaf school. In his adult life, like my mother, I never saw him read a book, only the newspaper. All of this was a reflection on the world that had been created for them. The most that could be hoped for in caring families was the ability to lead them into some type of employment.

In Morris' case, the existence of a father and siblings who cared little for him or his deaf brother Harry, relegated them to a position of servitude. They now lived on a farm where Morris and Harry were awakened at three A.M. to milk the cows and then work the farm for the remainder of the day. This, while the remainder of the siblings and father did little or nothing. Morris and Harry were definitely non-persons until they ran away from home.

Diana came from a much kinder family, which sought to find a place for her. Through a friend they found employment for her doing piece work in a millinery factory which took no particular skill. Diana, obviously very bright as well, rejected that. She wanted something more stimulating. Once again through a friend they got her job as a comptometer operator. But the department store that hired her, Lit Brothers, realized she was a minor and not sufficiently educated. They placed her for six months in their in-store school in order to be able to work there. She continued to work at Lit Brothers Department Store until they were married.

With that type of background, in searching for goals, they found it in their children. Somehow blessed with two above average children, they dreamt of great accomplishments for both the two of them. Their pride was hardly hidden. In Diana's case none of her siblings had gone beyond High School. In Morris' family it was the same, but worse in one way. His siblings were so mean they were certain nothing worthwhile could be possible in this world for children of the deaf as they treated him and Harry with disdain.

As the years passed their first son, my brother Arthur, with great financial difficulties made his way toward becoming an attorney. Great pride developed in them. Then as I began making educational strides, they began hoping that I would become a physician. In their eyes what greater thing could happen than to have this handicapped couple produce a doctor and a lawyer, when those around them thought so little of their abilities. Unfortunately, it appeared as if I would become a thorn in their dreams. In my defense, let me explain.

I was never a bad child. I never got into any trouble. I was loving, respectful and from the earliest age possible I followed in the footsteps of my older brother in trying to help them navigate society. We would make telephone calls for them, speak as an intermediary by phone, or in person, when problems arose. Though we were still children we did whatever was necessary to help them. Not doing that would be a sign of abject selfishness. These were two individuals who showed us nothing but constant love.

When Arthur went into the military, I was only 13 and assumed that role myself. Like my brother, I never felt that it was a burden. In fact, in later life I came to realize it was a blessing. I was being taught to accept responsibility at a very young age. It would always serve me well. So, what did I do to upset the applecart?

Somewhere around the age of 16 the problem began. In all the years up until that time I had the most minimal exposure to acting. I believe I once had a role in a play in elementary school.

I watched a show on television called something like COLLEGE BOWL. There was no such thing as video. Everything was live without recording. It was only 1949. Though I have no explanation for why or how, even living in a house with no music all my childhood years, I was seriously in love with music. It was primarily Broadway music that I adored.

In my mind the TV show was totally amateurish. I was certain I could do what they did and do it better. I knew absolutely no one in show business, but that did not deter me. Afterall, I was 16 years old. How could I possibly be wrong about anything? So I went, uninvited, to the offices of Donn Bennett Productions which produced the show. It was a type of variety show where "college students" went to a soda fountain, and broke into song and dance routines. There was a significant difference between the cast of the show and me. They were all trained singers, dancers and actors. But I was not concerned.

At the front desk sat a woman. She might have been somewhat surprised when I introduced myself and explained the reason I was there.

"I would like to become a member of your cast."

"What can you do?" she inquired.

"Everything! I sing. I dance. I act." Years later, during my second marriage, when my wife heard me give a similar response with no semblance of reality, she told me, "I never knew someone with so much "Chutzbah." (A Yiddish word describing over-the top self-aggrandizement.

The front desk receptionist was intelligent enough not to take me seriously. But something else caused her to then ask me to read something for her. Within a day or two I was contacted and told I was being hired to do television commercials on the program. The explanation was simple. Philadelphians had a terribly grating speech pattern. I had spent my entire life speaking slowly and clearly so my parents could understand me. It made me the perfect person for them to hire. I spent the next five plus years devoting every moment of my life to show business as an untrained, unskilled performer. So, it seems clear to me that the speech pattern I learned from them almost destroyed my life. I could always blame them if I became a nere-do-well performer.

The relationship I had with our parents was over-the-top special. I can only speak for myself, but I believe fairly certainly Arthur felt the same way. In their eyes I was the greatest thing since sliced bread. I always felt they expected great things from me. In my case it meant I had an obligation not to disappoint them. That must have made my brief and unsuccessful venture into show business very stressful for them.

I adored my father and my memories of my early years were so special. My father went to work dressed in a suit and tie every day. There were paint stains all over his suit. He was obviously not able to drive a car so he traveled by public transportation on the trolley car which stopped one block from our home. He carried with him a large heavy box, like a suitcase, which contained all the equipment he needed for his work. I don't remember ever seeing him leave, probably because it was before I left for school. But sometime, when I was about seven or eight years of age, I was allowed to walk the block between our house and the trolley stop at the time he was expected to return from work. It was certainly a time quite different from today. I was allowed to walk that block alone, which was dark by the time he was arriving in the winter, with no restriction. When I got to the corner where the trolley stopped, I would wait, sitting on the curb, with great anticipation every time a new trolley arrived, in the hope that my father would disembark. Then I would run to him and the two of us would greet each other with much love and walk hand in hand the block back to our house. I am certain I felt no person in the world had a grander life. I had no understanding I was living in the slums of Philadelphia.

Today, it often seems quite humorous when people tell me that they imagine it must have been a very difficult childhood with two deaf parents. My response to them is always the same. My childhood was glorious.

What makes the childhood experience of a young boy or girl unpleasant is the absence of love. Children who live in a world of abusive parents, or meanness and cruelty are the ones who have terrible experiences in their growing up years. I lived in a world of boundless love from my parents, my maternal grandparents, my brother, my cousin Bud and aunts and uncles. Well, maybe it was not so from my brother. He would tell me when we grew up that he had experienced all the normal feelings a sibling has when a second child suddenly comes on the scene. "Do I really need this interloper, when before him I had all this love just for me?" But he was a loving brother. I believe he would describe his childhood in the same way I did for myself.

Poverty has no meaning for a child as long as that child is well fed and dressed. Being able to have all that love and go to school and play in the street with friends after school is what matters to a child, not wealth.

I frankly believe that my childhood was not just acceptable even with their handicap. There is absolutely no way it could have been better.

CHAPTER FOUR
CHILDHOOD

When Morris was sent to Deaf School, Miss (The form Ms. was not yet in use) Garrett was the Principal. His teacher was Miss Zane. He was apparently one of the youngest students there. Subsequently, Miss Dalsemer taught him. There was one thing that did not vary among the three of them. They all loved him and believed he was remarkable. It was for that reason they selected him to be one of that very small group of students who would be paraded around the country to demonstrate what a deaf child, lip reading and not using sign language, was capable of accomplishing. He was nine years old when he was a part of that group. Through these children they hoped to get more Federal funding for deaf education by way of lip-reading.

All my repeated searches for information about his life at the school always came to a dead end. I went there several times. The schools had moved and apparently had records accidently destroyed, I was repeatedly told. It seemed quite unbelievable that this child who spent more than ten years in the Deaf School was for all intents and purposes without a single record of his existence. Had I not obtained information from Miss Dalsemer, my mother and the White House, it would seem that Morris Keyser never existed. It was not just the Deaf School that had no record of him. Bethlehem Steel, where he had worked for two years had no record whatsoever. The same would be true for Lehigh University. They would all claim there had been fires, inadvertent destruction of records and other strange reasons for the absence of records. It is difficult to understand why. Possibly the "lack of importance" of keeping track of the handicapped was a factor. Whatever the reason I was placed in a position of trying to reconstruct a story mainly by interviews and what I could find at The Library of Congress.

At approximately age eleven he was started in the public school system in Philadelphia at the Francis Reed School. When he reached the seventh grade, he was transferred to the Charles S. Close School. Shortly after that the family moved to the farm in New Jersey. He attended the Westend School in Franklinville, NJ. Morris was not allowed by his parents to remain there long enough to graduate.

At a speech given by Mary Garrett to the Annual Meeting of the New Jersey Congress of Mothers she related all this information about Morris and ended saying, "In all of these schools he succeeded in class with all hearing children." I have no exact record but interviews revealed that, ultimately, he was brought back to the farm. Harry was brought back as well. Morris and Harry from that point on became the work horses of the family on the farm where they now lived in Elmer, New Jersey.

At around age fourteen he had appendicitis. It is true that at that time, before antibiotics, appendicitis was not an uncommon cause of death. He was hospitalized for three weeks and did not return to normal for several months.

On the farm Morris at times was so discontented he would leave and walk back to Philadelphia to visit his beloved teachers and a Rabbi where his father had sent him to go to Sunday School. He was Rabbi Henry Berkowitz of the Rodeph Shalom Congregation, in Philadelphia. Morris was so scantily clothed. He wore shoes without leather soles, just cardboard. Like everyone else Rabbi Berkowitz was completely enamored of Morris and would provide him with shoes and warmer clothes.

At first, the Rabbi was afraid that a deaf child would hold back the hearing children. In 1913 when Morris was seventeen, Rabbi Berkowitz wrote the following letter to Mary Garrett.

"It affords me great pleasure to assure you that our experience with Morris Keyser, who received his training at your school, demonstrated his perfect ability to carry on the work in the religious school in our congregation. He entered the Confirmation Class and prepared his studies the same as the other pupils. He got quite a fair knowledge of the Hebrew language and ranks among the best in all subjects. I am informed by the instructor of the Confirmation Class that he is one of the most capable members. At first, I thought he might interfere with the progress. But to the contrary he stimulated the less gifted pupils who had no such limitations under which he suffered."

"I want to say that one of the finest effects of his presence in the class was a moral influence exerted upon the other pupils that manifested itself in many gracious ways and brought out the finer traits of his classmates. It affords me much satisfaction to give you this testimony and wishing you every success, Henry Berkowitz."

Morris was seventeen years of age at that time.

Morris had a brother named Simon. Like the rest of Morris' siblings, with the exception of Harry his deaf younger brother and Barney, he generally treated Morris as a non-person. But that was not the only Simon in his life. Shortly after our father died, I had the great good fortune to interview Morris' cousin Simon and his wife.

Morris's parents, Anna and Sam, were also cousins. Though that is not legal today, it was a common practice at that time.

Morris' mother had a sister who married the father of his cousin Simon Keyser. So this Simon Keyser was actually Morris' first cousin. He was just 11 months younger than Morris and grew up on the same street, Rodman Street, in Philadelphia. He saw a different person in Morris than our father's siblings did. They were bosom buddies who would spend a great deal of time together, like going to the silent movies. Simon marveled at the kind of person Morris was. Simon said, "I never met anybody from childhood to manhood who disliked him or that he disliked. I never heard anybody who didn't say he was a great guy. That's the God's honest truth."

"Like his mother he was very warm."

Simon's wife told me that they were the only ones on Morris' side of the family invited to our parents' wedding. Simon said they were more like brothers than cousins. Simon was constantly impressed with what Morris was able to accomplish even with his handicap.

Whenever the two of them stopped to get something to eat, our father would insist on paying for it. "He was like that. He'd never let me pay. He was like that," Simon said.

Simon didn't think very much of Morris' family. He recalled when Morris' sister Fanny passed away, he saw her brother Louie having a meal at Horn and Hardart's Automat during the ceremony, having not been invited to the funeral.

Simon could only be described as being effusive in his praise for the type of man Morris was, a wonderful son, husband and father. He once met Morris on a downtown street and asked where he was going. Morris told him he was going to an office building to put his son Arthur's name on the door for his first position as a lawyer. Morris would not let Simon go on his way. He insisted Simon come and see him do it because he was so proud of Arthur.

There were many touching stories he revealed to me. Two involved times when he saw Morris begin to cry. One was when they were children. Harry was having frequent epileptic seizures. In one incident it happened out on the street. It was so ferocious that Harry ended up with multiple cuts and bruises on his face and head from striking the sidewalk. Morris cried as he held him.

The second time was much later when Morris had a stroke near the end of his life. Simon visited him in the hospital. He walked to the side of the bed where our father could still move his hand.

Morris grasped Simon leg with his arm and began to cry. Simon said he began crying as well.

But of all the stories he told, none pleased me more than this one. When Morris' family became even more destitute, they decided to move to the country. Morris, a young teenager, asked Simon to do him an important favor. In the past Simon had seen the silver engraved ashtray that Morris had received from President Theodore Roosevelt. Morris had no idea what might happen to it during the move and asked Simon, "Will you keep it safe for me while I am gone?"

Simon then revealed that sometime much later he realized he had lost this treasure and was so embarrassed he never spoke about it to Morris again. Up to the time of my interview with him, when our father had already passed away, Simon had felt terrible guilt and finally revealed it to me. But the truth was that sometime after Morris came back to Philadelphia, Simon had returned the ash tray to our father and had not recalled he had done that. As a result, he carried that guilt for the remainder of his life because he loved Morris so much.

One cannot imagine the joy he expressed when I revealed to him that it was not so. My father still retained the gift and had passed it on to me, and it was safely in my possession.

In the chronology of Morris' life, soon World War 1 began. Morris obviously was not eligible to be a member of the armed services. Nevertheless, three times he attempted to enlist. Of course, he was always rejected.

He had known about the existence of Bethlehem Steel. Sometime, when he was in his early twenties, he attempted to get a job there. The work was extremely dangerous even for a non-handicapped person, so he was turned down in the same manner the Army had rejected him. But, subsequently through some maneuver, he snuck into the plant and with the help of friends got hired.

He told me years later about the terrible dangers of that environment, where it was reported an average of six workers died in accidents every two weeks. It was easy to understand from the descriptions my father gave me as I was growing up. Molten steel ingots were tossed from employee to employee, caught with some gadget they held in their hands. You can imagine the danger to a deaf person who could not hear the warning if the toss was off target. It is at this point in the story that I faced a major problem. Wherever I could, I tried to verify every story in his life with more than one source. Now I was confronted with a story that my father had never told me, which seemed amazing, because he would describe so many things to me with great detail. It was complicated by the fact that I had interviewed our mother multiple times and had detailed printed documents of everything she revealed about our Dad. There were many minimal details which were not significant and never included in this biography. They were not offensive or destructive to the story I will tell. They are not in the story because they were such mundane bits of information. They would have no value. But I refer to them here, because it is difficult to imagine she would leave out the story I am about to tell if she had ever been aware of it. So why not just leave it out of the book and never refer to it. The simple reason is that the story was told to me by my brother which made me feel it could not be ignored. To my knowledge he never lied to me about anything all during my long ninety years of life. This is what he told me our father told him.

In order to understand this story, it is necessary to understand the nature of my father's handicap during all the years I knew him. As opposed to our mother, who was one hundred percent deaf from the moment of her death, never hearing a single sound from the moment of her birth, my father heard some sounds. We never had a telephone in our house. It was different for him at work.

In 1920, years before he began to work for Alexander Larmour only one third of businesses in America possessed a telephone. By the mid 1920 when he started, I imagine that number had risen considerably. But in his position as a painting employee, he had no reason to be on a telephone. As the years passed by and Larmour became incapacitated, our father became the individual who ran the entire company. He was the person making arrangements with clients, computing the estimates for the jobs, hiring the people to work under him. He was the boss who did everything. Whatever year that began Morris had to talk on the phone every day.

Putting a phone next to his ear, essentially a microphone, was not dissimilar to the methodology we use today with hearing aids. So people who can barely hear, or discern what is spoken around them, are able to hear what is said on a telephone. That is apparently what existed for him. Without a telephone he was relegated back to lip reading when in conversation with anyone. But another thing was critical for him. Having heard some sounds he was able to reproduce them in his speech so that he was not afflicted with the strange dissonant speech generally heard from the deaf who have never heard, like our mother.

The story my brother told me related to the time our father was at Bethlehem Steel. As Arthur told it, our father was profoundly deaf all during his childhood, hearing absolutely nothing. At Bethlehem Steel he unfortunately was the victim of an accident which knocked him unconscious. When he awakened, he suddenly found that he had gained for the first time the minimal hearing we all knew him to have in adult life. I was in a quandary about presenting this as factual information in the book.

I began to seek the help from audiologists to determine if that was possible. The answer remained constant, "No!"

Was there some explanation? Their interpretation was that our father always had the minimal hearing he possessed in adult life.

There were no telephones that he used as a child or young adult. When he began using the telephone, he realized he could hear that amount which allowed him to communicate and used lip reading when not on the phone.

So that is the story I had to tell. I leave it to the reader to decide whether the story is true or apochryphal, as are so many amazing stories told in biographies and even more so in autobiographies.

The other stories I knew from his time at Bethlehem Steel I am certain were true, because they would not be something that one might be proud of or brag about. All the years I was old enough to understand the adult world around me, our father was a teetotaler. He never drank. Our mother told me of an incident that was so rare she never forgot it. Once when there were plans for him to come home from work early on a Saturday, she waited for hours without him appearing. Some of his friends from work asked him to have just one drink with them before leaving. They plied him with drink after drink until he was so drunk, they had to cart him home. Diana, our mother was furious. As she told the story, when he awoke she laid into him and it was never repeated.

But when he was just in his early twenties, long before he met her, things were different. He had a job at Bethlehem Steel. He had no other obligations. On Friday night when work ended, he spent the entire weekend with friends drunk until Monday morning. That was his life, week after week. But when married that would happen just once the remainder of his life.

While at Bethlehem his foreman, Mr. Schwab, was so impressed with him that he made arrangements to get a scholarship for him at Lehigh University to learn about blueprints. After working in the daytime, he attended Lehigh at night. After a few weeks he left because they were completely unprepared to teach a deaf person and he was unable to understand anything. The instructor spoke facing the blackboard with his back toward Morris.

During that period of his life, not unlike a number of deaf men, he sought a career as a prize fighter. I know that did not last long. Though when I knew him in his late thirties and forties he was in excellent physical condition and very muscular. However, it did not help him as a boxer. My assumption is he had little success, possibly never winning a match. It was not a surprise to me. He could hardly be successful at that. He had no killer instinct.

When the war ended, he left Bethlehem Steel and moved in with a hearing friend, Robert Young, for three years. Young was a radio engineer. With earphones, he taught Morris how to understand words. It was a wonderful relationship that finally ended when Robert got married.

All the time Morris was at Bethlehem Steel and through his twenties he would send money back to his parents who faced economic difficulties and ultimately gave up the farm and returned to live in Philadelphia. With all the terrible things they did to him while he growing up, Morris continued to show love and respect for them as they grew older. It was probably mostly because of the love he had for and from his mother.

Our father then got a job with a painting contractor Wilson and Co. It was 1922 and Morris was twenty-six years old. In November of that year Wilson sent a letter to Mary Garrett, principal of the Deaf School.

"My Dear Miss Garrett:

We are very glad to be given the opportunity to tell you of the remarkable success of training given by your school to Morris Keyser, one of our employees.

While deaf, it is no handicap to him. He can (match) employees. He is alert and always ready to execute any orders.

As a mechanic, he is very successful being a willing worker, very much interested in his calling. *He cannot help but be successful in life and is equal to any employee and superior to many.*
Yours very truly,
James S. Wilson"

Morris' boss there was Alexander Larmour. Larmour decided to quit working for Wilson and opened his own sign shop. He asked Morris to come work for him, and our Dad agreed.

Soon after that our Dad was confronted with a major problem. He was very shy when it came to his social life and rarely went out on dates. Some deaf friends from Allentown encouraged him to join them on a trip to New York to meet some deaf girls. One of them asked Morris to stay overnight at her apartment. He refused, left and returned to Philadelphia. A few days later he received a letter and a box of fruit from her. The letter stated she was wearing an engagement ring he had given to her. He was very angry but did nothing. A few days later he received another letter saying she was suing him for breach of promise. Morris took the letter to Alexander Larmour's devoted secretary. She wrote a strong letter to this woman in New York for Morris. She was never heard from again.

Larmour must have been a very fine artist in his own right, because he taught our father so much that ultimately there was no one else in Philadelphia of his caliber. It was unbelievable as Morris had been completely untrained when he met Alexander Larmour.

At some point, when Morris was well established, a number of terrible things happened. Larmour's devoted secretary for many years was killed in an automobile accident. Then Larmour's wife died of cancer after a long terrible illness. Larmour fell into a period of habitual drinking to the point of collapse. He probably had always been a heavy drinker. But this essentially ended his career. By then Morris could manage everything. He became responsible for retrieving him from stuporous states in bars, bringing him home and putting him to bed. It was all very stressful and depressing to Morris who truly loved Alexander Larmour for teaching him a career.

Larmour met a woman in a bar and married her. She was a strong woman who said she would take over the business. Larmour said "No! Morris will run the business." With the constant drinking it was a rocky marriage. At one point Larmour went to Ireland without her and lost, drinking and gambling, all the money he had with him. Finally, she left him and they got divorced, leaving Morris to take care of him through all his alcoholic binges.

In 1941 when my brother Arthur was 12 years old, our Dad brought him into the shop after school and on Saturday to help answer the phone and take message for him while he was out working. By then fifteen years had passed since Alex and Morris began working together. Ultimately, our Dad arranged for Alex's daughter Anne to come work answering the phone. By then Larmour was in and out of the hospital with cirrhosis of the liver. Morris changed the sign on the window to say Alexander Larmour and Company. He was always devoted to Alex, feeling it was Larmour's business. Morris always considered himself an employee just working for a salary. But our mother Diana was resentful because Morris worked so hard and received a minimal salary, the remainder all going to Larmour. Though Alex was always good to Morris, it is probably true, the reason Morris remained at or not far above the poverty range was at least partially related to the fact that he was deaf. The handicapped have always been treated as if they were second class citizens.

However, an amazing thing happened after Larmour died. When Alex's will was read, his family was shocked. They had not been rejected by their father, but Morris was named a one fourth owner of Alexander Larmour and Company. It made a major difference in the lives of our parents.

CHAPTER FIVE
THE COURTSHIP

Diana saw Morris for the first time when she was about nine or ten years old. Morris frequently returned to the school to see his teachers who adored him. That first sighting came at Christmas time when Morris, at the request of the teachers, dressed as Santa Claus. He would have been nineteen or twenty years old. As time passed, she saw him occasionally when he returned to the school for visits. She had not seen him for some time, since she left deaf school at age 15, when a deaf friend of Morris said he wanted to introduce him to her. I don't think that meeting ever occurred. But Morris knew who she was.

Then a hearing young woman, Diana knew from her job at Lit Brothers, told her about a deaf man who lived next door to her. She said he was wonderful. They then communicated with some notes before Morris decided to go see her in person.

When he arrived, he was greeted at her house by one of her parents and introduced himself. He inquired if she was at home. As it turned out Diana was out on one of her constant dates. This time it was with the most prominent Jewish prize fighter in Philadelphia. Prize fighting was a promising career for a young deaf man in a world where not many opportunities existed for the handicapped. If you were good, the remuneration was very attractive. And Diana, considered quite beautiful, was a woman these young men wanted to have on their arms.

She had dated this prize fighter before. As she told me in later years, she couldn't stand him. He was a show off who would seat her at a table alone while he circulated at the club, visiting with his friends.

Diana's father, who didn't like the men she was dating, asked Morris to come in and wait.

What came to pass was quite special. Morris sat and talked with Harry and Rose Rubin for more than two hours. They would say later that Morris was by far the nicest deaf man they had ever met who dated their daughter. Finally, Diana came home and they agreed to meet sometime in July.

They began seeing each other on a regular basis. By that time Morris was showing up at the Lit Brothers employee's exit every night when Diana's shift ended in order to take her home. Our mother said our father was always very shy and sweet. They were in love.

A date was set for December primarily for economic reasons. Diana's brother Herman was getting married to his fiancé Evelyn. The plan was for Herman and Evelyn to get married first and then Diana could wear Evelyn's wedding outfit. It worked out fine with the dress but Diana's shoe size was much larger than Evelyn's. As a result, Diana was in pain the entire wedding. Ater Morris and Diana married they went immediately to New York City for a honeymoon. Morris said the first thing they did was go to a shoe store to buy shoes for Diana.

After my father died my mother and I worked together on research to write this book. She quite openly discussed their sex life which she said was wonderful. I discovered it remained very active and frequent until just about two years before he died. It was limited then only because of his illness.

Their love story lasted 49 ½ years. During that time, I never heard our father ever raise his voice to her. But it wasn't as if there was little interaction. Sweet and kind were not the only aspects of his personality that existed between them. Our father had a wonderful sense of humor and would love to tease her in the effort to make her laugh. He would do silly things like hide in a closet and jump out as she looked for him. She described for me incidents like our father lying prone on the floor pretending to be ill or unconscious, only to jump up and laugh when she became frightened. She did not always appreciate his humor and would chastise him for his behavior. In fact she frequently became angry with him. But the result was aways the same. He never responded to her anger with reciprocal anger. He just tried to make her laugh and get over it. She told me it was impossible to maintain the exasperation and would finally get over her annoyance. He was too loveable to not give in to his kindness.

She was always unhappy about the cigar smoking. Her constant harangues about that finally achieved success when she absolutely insisted and he stopped on the dime. It wasn't a factor of health that made our mother so upset. At that time there was probably little knowledge of the dangers of smoking.

Morris was a strange type of smoker. He lit a cigar the moment he began to work. But after a puff or two he stopped. The flame went out and he continued to keep the cigar hanging out the side of his mouth, chewing away like it was chewing tobacco. I never once saw him spit as tobacco chewers do. He probably just swallowed the juice. But the sloppiness of it was what offended Diana. I don't know what caused the culmination of the habit, but I am aware of one situation, long before he stopped, that drove her to distraction.

Morris had a very strong work ethic which I will describe in a later chapter. He never wanted to take any vacation time. But that did not affect what he wanted for Diana and his children, all three of whom he adored.

In the nineteen thirties when Arthur and I were very young and there was no money for actual vacations, we would all go on frequent one day trips to Atlantic City. That resort was only sixty miles from Philadelphia. We would pack our beach clothes, beach toys and lunch and all get on the trolley car to the downtown train station in Philadelphia. We then took the train to Atlantic City and walked from there to the beach. We would go into the public bathrooms there to change into our bathing suits and find a spot to settle in for the entire day. In my memory it was glorious, running back and forth from that beach blanket to the ocean with our mother right behind shouting, "Don't go out to far." From the number of times she was certain we would drown, I am amazed that my 95 year old brother and I are still alive.

Our mother had packed our lunch with all our favorites which we consumed with gusto. Then as the sun began to set we began our sad trek in the opposite direction from where we had started the day, while wishing the day would never end. We made our way back to the train station where the train always remained standing for a while before leaving. Our father disembarked saying he was going to the kiosk in the station to buy a cigar for the trip. It was a time when smoking on the train was completely accepted. But just after he got off the train, it started and left the station. Our father was not on board. I was probably only about six years old, so I don't remember how we made it home with our mother alone caring for us, but we did. I'm not even certain I remember this incident or whether what seems like my memory is just the many times I heard this story. I am told a long time passed before our mother's anger vanished. Nevertheless, ultimately, he gave up cigars.

But cigar smoking was the only area where he resisted her wishes. I believe that other than that, he ever denied her anything she wanted. Though he was a remarkable breadwinner, he did not run the family. It was absolutely matriarchal. Though Diana received absolutely no advice or direction about how to be a wife, there were some things she must have learned by osmosis. It was not as if she was ignored by her parents. Somehow, they were not able to recognize that she would need the same direction as a hearing child would receive. Diana was exposed to a family in which her mother was the matriarch, and set the example for her.

Diana would be responsible for all the decisions about the children, clothing, schools, etc. In my case, living eight blocks from my elementary school, she would walk that trip eight times every day, to school, back to pick me up for lunch, back after lunch and then at the end of the day, sometimes in the rain.

She handled all the finances of our family. On Friday evening Morris would give Diana all the proceeds of his earnings. Every day she provided him with sufficient money to cover the cost of his transportation, lunch and probably one or two cigars, which were only five cents each as he "smoked" and chewed the dregs of the cigar market. I believe it was three dollars each day he received. That number may have changed with time. It never occurred to him to spend any money to purchase anything for himself.

After they were married Morris told Diana about some of the girls in Philadelphia he dated during his twenties. They were all deaf. Several were extremely wealthy. One was a daughter from the Potamkin family. They owned a large fish business. But the most affluent was the Buten family who owned one of the largest paint manufacturing companies in the U.S. Our mother Diana knew both these young women from her days at the deaf school. In my interview with her she freely told me that one was very nice, but the other was not. I will not reveal which was which.

After they were married, they would frequently meet some of them at deaf functions. In one case they met a woman Morris had dated who was unhappily married. She asked Morris if he would begin to take her out again, even though she knew he was married.

Dad walking us through downtown Philadelphia.

He is ten and I am six. He is considerably taller
Three years later we are the same height.

Arthur with our Dad when he was in the Army

My high school graduation photo.

Dad at the seashore, always in his suit, not a bathing suit. But he does have his trusty cigar.

Our mother Diana with her older brother Herman who died very young and her younger brother Sam. Her baby sister Pauline was not yet born.

Our maternal grandparents Rose and Harry Rubin.

CHAPTER SIX
RECOLLECTIONS

No child has the same relationship with a parent that another of his or her siblings will experience. That is the reason they all turn out differently. Arthur, being more than four years older than I, certainly experienced things of which I was never a part. He recalled our father taking him to an extravaganza in a stadium called a military tattoo. It was comprised of many bands and marching soldiers. Arthur remembered it as being glorious and going on until about 3 A.M. I was either not yet born or very young. Even Arthur must have been very young. He recalled that he did not want to leave because it was so exciting. He and our father stayed, and stayed and stayed.

Meanwhile, our mother was in a panic as the hours went on. When they returned, she was furious with our Dad. Arthur's explanation was that our father would do almost anything to make us happy.

In our discussions, Arthur described a huge difference in the personalities of our parents. Morris was out in the world of business and dealt with business people all the time. Diana was sheltered and had none of those experiences. Even with that, she had a much more realistic view of the world. Morris seemed so naïve. He never perceived any person in a negative way. He saw only goodness in everyone and could not remain in a room where the conversation was condemning of anyone. He would just leave.

Arthur recalled a birthday celebration for our maternal grandmother. It was a big party because she had just recovered from a serious illness. After she blew out the birthday candles, each of her children and grandchildren who were there came to her to give a perfunctory kiss on her cheek. Morris came over, hugged her for a long time and both began to cry.

It reminded me of an incident I experienced with the same grandmother. It was at a time when I had already reached adult life. My maternal Grandma Rose decided to tell me something that she wanted to be certain I knew. In the privacy of just the two of us, she said that her very best child (She had given birth to four) was my father. The first thing that struck me was that my father was not her child. He was her son-in-law.

From Arthur I learned Larmour was constantly drunk. Our father not only ran the business, he cared for Larmour as if he was his nurse. Never once did it occur to our father to leave him and start his own shop. He just continued to work as an employee, taking out his meager salary and giving the rest to Larmour. He was the premier painter in Philadelphia. There was no sign painter and gilder equal to him in all of Philadelphia. The business was all our father. He was the attraction.

When Larmour died and left one quarter of the business to Dad. That was a farce. These three natural children of Larmour contributed nothing to the business. Our father should have received 100%.

But Morris saw nothing bad in that and continued to work for them. He was always happy, never sad and cared nothing for material things. That attitude would frequently anger our Mother who could get annoyed with his total acceptance of the status quo, but he would always defuse it by teasing her. He would never stop until she gave in and began to laugh. She loved him and showed it. Diana was the head of our matriarchal family, but always wanted to make him feel as if he were king.

His working hours were very irregular. As a result, he would come home late at times. Dinner would never begin until he got home. He was always covered in paint. The first thing he would do was go up to the bathroom and scrub down with harsh Lava soap. He was always a very clean and fastidious person. Only then would dinner begin.

On those rare occasions we went out to eat, although she had all the money, she never paid the bill. She would give him the money so that he would pay it. She wanted him to feel that he was in charge.

I remember if I did something that made Mother angry, she would threaten to tell our Dad, in the hope that the threat would make us behave. But it was nonsense, because Dad would never punish us. I don't remember him ever punishing us and certainly never striking us. I remember our mother spanking us in the most minimal way, but never our father.

On rare occasions they would go to the Deaf Club. But Morris never liked going there. I think he only went to please our mother. He seemed to be so much happier with the hearing population. I think he never saw himself as being handicapped. But because his hearing was so limited, when he spoke, he constantly mispronounced words. He didn't misuse them as in malapropism, he just did not know what they really sounded like. (I can recall any time he and I would go for a hamburger at Burger King, he would ask me to order a Whooper for him.)

When he was younger, he could sit with a pencil and piece of paper and sketch anything for me. (Not a single scrap of such drawings remains today. They were never saved.)

But it could be seen in his handwriting. It was the most beautiful I had ever seen. He had such a fluid motion with his hand. Morris had a nephew Gerson who was one of the few really nice people on his side of the family. Gerson spent his entire life as a successful artist. He made a wonderful career out of his painting, receiving quite large payments for his work. I am aware of at least one of his paintings being sold at Sotheby's, and possibly there were others. His wife Evelyn was an equally successful artist. Because Gerson died so young at the age of 62, Evelyn's career continued for almost a quarter of a century after his death. She was a sculptor who worked in wood, leaving many of her art objects present in a number of collections.

Gerson told me, after our father's death, if Dad had the opportunity to be a fine artist, not a commercial artist, he would have been extremely successful, which of course we will never know.

Uncle Barney was an important part of our lives. Of all the Keyser children, Morris and Barney were the only ones who helped their parents financially. Though Morris was earning very little money, he gave 25% of it to his parents. When they moved into the house they rented where we lived as children, the monthly rental was $28. Barney was the only one who was professionally success. He was a teletype operator for the local radio station that transmitted the action of the local baseball team, the Philadelphia Athletics. He earned a very fine salary.

It was a different world from the television we know of today. Uncle Barney, watching the game in the stadium would teletype a message to the station of the visiting team. He was not a writer or an analyst. He just operated the teletype equipment. He would send the message such as strike, ball, home run, etc. On the other end the announcer, who was a professional sportscaster, would tell his listeners in the distant city a completely made-up story. It took considerable talent to perform his job to perfection.

'The pitcher winds up. Here comes a fast ball. The batter takes a ferocious swing and misses it. Strike one.' All Uncle Barney had sent him was, 'Strike One'. The announcer would construct a scenario that would keep the listener glued to the radio broadcast.

Barney was living with us and paid our parents seven dollars a week rent. Simple computation shows that the entire rental for the house for the four of us and Barney was paid for by Barney.

Previously I related the story of our excursions for a single weekend day to Atlantic City. Arthur told me how that had changed.

One day Barney said to his brother (our father), he was not going to watch these children stay at home all summer. They need to go to Atlantic City for at least two weeks. Dad said that was a wonderful idea but he didn't have the money to pay for it. Barney told him he would pay for it and did for two summers until Dad was able to pay for it himself.

Uncle Barney was always very kind and loved Morris and Diana. He was pretty crazy about us kids as well. Every Sunday we knew when we heard him come out of his room to the top of the stairs, he would take all the change out of his pocket, throw it down the stairs and watch us scramble for it. Barney was the economic force that saved us during the Depression."

Uncle Barney had a girlfriend named Lizzie. I met her several times but never knew her well. She had a child, which rumor had it, that Barney had fathered. I met her at some time during those years, but I was probably too young to understand that Uncle Barney was her father.

He lived with us continually until I was twelve years old. All I can remember was he was the first person I ever knew who died. I didn't know him to ever have an illness. I just remember he died sitting in the chair that was always his in the living room.

The one thing that sticks in my mind is that at age twelve it was the saddest day I had ever known. I had never been exposed to death. I loved Uncle Barney and he was gone.

CHAPTER SEVEN
MORRIS AND WORK

There is no chapter more important or more descriptive of the inner soul of Morris Keyser. In an interview with my older brother Arthur, he told me,

"He was one of the happiest persons I have ever known in my life. He got so much pleasure out of everything. He got pleasure out of going to work. He got pleasure out of walking on the street with his box and paints in his hands. He would say 'hello' to the people he met. He was a happy person all the time."

It all began in his early twenties. He had completed his time during World War 1 working at Bethlehem Steel. It is clear that he then faced a world in which he had no adequate education and no known skills. When the war ended the need for massive amounts of steel soon ended. As would be expected the last employees, who were hired due to the war needs, would soon be laid off.

It appears through some source he started working for a painting contractor named Wilson. Wilson had, as part of his force of employees, a sign painter Alexander Larmour. Alexander had taken a liking to the young, bright deaf man who seemed to be able to do whatever was asked of him. Larmour was unhappy with his arrangement at Wilson and decided he would open up his own sign shop. He asked Morris if he would be willing to quit Wilson and work for him and learn about sign painting. Morris agreed and a powerful relationship, that would last as long as Larmour survived, began.

I suspect that Alexander Larmour was quite a fine artist in his own right. I can't imagine it could be otherwise as his protégé became the finest sign painter in probably the entire east coast.

In the beginning, our Dad told me, he just mixed paints. Then Larmour began to teach him about gilding.

Gold lettering is an exquisite art form executed in the following manner. Whatever one desires to paint, it is first done with an almost colorless liquid called 'size.' After it is all painted, and almost invisible, the artist then impresses against the 'size' very thin sheets of paper which have on their surface gold leaf. The gold leaf is so thin that if accidently touched by a finger will melt and vanish away. That may sound impossible and an exaggeration. I can tell you it is absolutely factual because as a naughty child, when I had the opportunity I would place my finger on the gold, and whoops, it would be gone. It takes the most skilled craftsman to be able to hold the sheets of paper, on the side without the gold, and manipulate them. The sheet is then lightly pressed against size on the glass or wood. The size has a gluelike nature that attracts the gold from the sheet without melting it, leaving a golden image where it has attached. The attachment demands a pressure on the paper which I cannot quantify, since I have never done it. I can only describe what I saw our father do. He pressed on the paper on the non-gold side with his right thumb, in such a manner that the gold was left behind on the glass with not the slightest defect. He would continue to do that with each letter.

Before describing the remainder of the process, I must describe a physical feature of Morris that I retained forever in my memory. When individuals describe a feature of a love one, it might commonly be "beautiful blue eyes," "lovely reddish hair that fell gently over her shoulders" or something to that nature." There is nothing like that in the memory I have of our father. It is the distal phalanx of his right thumb that will always remain in my memory. It had become absolutely perpendicular to the middle phalanx. It was not slightly bent out, but perpendicular. It was that finger that he constantly pressed against the paper holding the gold, to the surface to which he was transferring the gold. It had become permanently bent.

He had learned to do that from Larmour. He had reached a position so special that no one in Philadelphia, who was going to have his name placed on a door as a new lawyer, new accountant or any professional occupying an office, would want it to be done by anyone other than Morris Keyser. Ultimately, that would present problems. Over the years, the firm Alexander Larmour would gain control of every office building and a huge number of companies which would exclusively utilize their services. Really what these clients wanted was not employees of Alexander Larmour, but Morris Keyser. When it reached a point of having as many as six sign painters working for Morris, it was difficult to persuade clients to allow those other than Morris to appear on the job.

As was made clear earlier, Alexander Larmour's life went into complete dissolution. The result was that Morris gradually took over running the entire operation. Not only was he the principal painter, he was the business manager as well. He was taking the calls and agreeing to take the jobs. He was the estimator for what the job was worth and how much should be charged. Every job was different and required someone who understood how many man hours it would take, what the additional expenditures were (rent, phone, electricity, insurance, etc.), and what profit margin needed to be then calculated. How he learned all that, with no training at all in how to run a commercial enterprise, is totally beyond anything I can imagine. But he did it all successfully.

The problem of persuading clients to use other painters was not something easily accomplished. To understand the difficulty, one needed to realize the difference in the different painters. The others, besides our father, would have the assignment to paint in gold leaf the name on the door. They would line up the top and bottom of the line on which it was to appear. Then they tried to space it so that the name would be centered. How they did this varied from one to another. There was also the factor of what the gold surface on each letter would be like, perfect or maybe almost perfect. Sometimes they were successful and sometimes not. I'm not certain of the frequency, but at times Morris needed to correct the job.

Watching Morris was amazing. He had a trick he did with a piece of string and a ball of chalk. He would rub the length of the string several times across the chalk. Place the string with his left hand against the glass window at a point he selected just by sight. It was without measurement. He then did a trick flicking the string with his right hand against the glass. It left a single line of chalk that was perfectly parallel to the ground with no measurement. He would then look at the name to be painted. Once again with no measurement he would begin painting the name and somehow always have it centered on the window. Once I was old enough to understand, as an adult, there was nothing magical about it. It was my career in Medicine that helped me understand.

I came to understand that there were many people who had achieved similar feats. There apparently exists a natural phenomenon in people who lose some of their senses. Other senses that survive frequently become more powerful. I realized that the loss of hearing had made the sense of sight in him much stronger than in those who maintained all their senses. You could tell it not just in his work, but in his conversations. He would love walking all over downtown with my brother, and with me when I got older. The conversations we had eighty years ago are as vivid to me as if they occurred yesterday. He would point to a sign on a billboard or in windows and say to me, "Herbie do you see that "S"? It is too close to the letter next to it!"

One thing that I will absolutely never forget was his "paint box." It was made so perfectly for him. It may very well have been built by him. If not, he purchased an item that perfectly fit his needs. It was a box made of wood shaped like a miniature suitcase. When it was opened by releasing the hinges on top it opened into a sort of cabinet with small shelves, drawers and cabinets. Each one held different supplies he needed to do his work, multiple brushes, tubes of paint, etc., etc.

There was one other item I can see in my mind's eye and never forget. It was something that he had created himself, not purchased. It was a long rod, made of wood and about two feet in length. It could be apparently separated in its center so that it would fit in his box. One end on the rod had a ball of some sort of fabric, about half the size of a baseball. It must have had something sticky or tacky on the fabric which allowed it to hold firmly when rested against glass. I previously mentioned that the only marking he made on the glass he was lettering was a single chalk line. But he had another trick. Our Dad will hold the long rod in his left hand at the end without the sticky fabric. He would then place the fabric end against the glass and rest his right forearm on the rod extending across the front of his body. In this way he would guarantee that while he painted his arm and hand would always be stable. Possibly others used the same trick. But to me it was magic.

I also remember the box, with all the supplies, was so heavy. I couldn't imagine how he lifted it. But for all the years that he worked he carried it around for great distances as he walked through the center of Philadelphia. One of the things that has stayed with me about the box was my mother's complaint. She would constantly state, about Alexander Larmour, that he was so cheap because he would never provide transportation, like a taxi, to get Morris from one job to another. Now the truth was that our father was running the business and making that decision himself. But, when I was older and a physician, I came to another understanding which I tried unsuccessfully to impress upon my mother. It was that the physical exercise of carrying that box all those years probably extended his life.

All of this came so natural to him. He could see things in his mind's eye with perfect clarity, that others could not. He had the eye of an artistic genius. It wasn't something only I realized. Everyone who called Alexander Larmour Sign Shop knew it and wanted only him. You might think he would notice that and think of himself as someone special. He was not capable of that. He saw nothing special in himself. It was just something that he did.

Those walks that our father did with us all through the center of Philadelphia I assume were not just to instruct us about the things we saw around us. He was well known in the center of the city by so many people. Every lawyer, every judge, every professional had had their names painted by him. It was said of him that he knew every judge and lawyer in town as well as every hobo. And even more important, he didn't know the difference and didn't care. None of them knew his name. But they would always greet him on the street with a "Hi! Deafy." It was not out of disrespect or cruelty. That was how they knew him.

He would stop to talk to each one of them for a very special reason. It was to tell them about the amazing person he had walking with him, "This my son (Arthur or Herbie)," He would brag about how marvelous these children, who had accomplished nothing, were. He got so much joy about showing his children to the world. He was an amazing father. But hardly an amazing disciplinarian. Neither Arthur nor I can recall being disciplined by him. His heart was too tender to ever allow him to do that. It had to be left to our mother.

I can say without the slight concern about whether it was truthful, our father did not know or understand the word hate. He would leave a conversation where hateful opinions were being professed.

It seems ridiculous to say he was a devoted husband and father. His love and pride in everything his wife and children did knew no bounds.

At his death our Aunt Pauline, our mother's sister, said "He was the most sweet and gentle man." She followed that by clarifying, "I say that not because he has died. When he was alive everyone who knew him, knew it."

But his gilding was not restricted to the names he painted throughout the center city. He gilded many beautiful outdoor structures like the animals on the dome of the Philadelphia Museum of Art which became iconic with the filming of "Rocky." He gilded the dome of the Inquirer Building, a sculpture museum in Philadelphia on the Parkway and a portion of the Franklin Institute. I never saw him do any of those iconic structures. But I have seen the pictures taken of him. He was high in the air, standing on scaffolding that had been built surrounding the area he would gild by hand. Some of the surfaces were quite large which must have necessitated him working out in the open, high above the ground, to complete the assignment. Ultimately, that would have an effect on him which I will describe later.

The work in the office buildings was so exclusively his, because the building superintendents made the arrangements for the clients about getting their names posted. They would refuse to allow any other gilders to come into the buildings to do the jobs, only Morris.

But it wasn't only the office buildings. Work came from painting contractors, schools, libraries, Hospitals, Universities, The Scott Paper Company, insurance companies, radio station WCAU, churches and the brick layer John B. Kelly. Our mother told us there were many more that she could not remember. It was also true that besides all these organizations in Philadelphia there were numerous jobs outside of the city. Everyone knew that Alexander Larmour Sign Shop, run by "deafy," was the place to have your work done.

Of all the gold leaf lettering I had seen him do, nothing was more remarkable in my mind than an assignment which boggled my mind. He was to paint the name of a restaurant on a window. It was to be painted on the inside of the window, which I assume was to protect it from the weather outside. The name was to be painted in script and on a diagonal across the window. This then required that he paint the name backward in script on the inside of the window, so that it could be seen as natural writing on the outside, where the customers would see it. There were several locations. This logo had to be the same in each one. To me it seemed unimaginable that anyone could do this with just the naked eye. I imagined how I would try to accomplish that if it were me. I thought I would paint it on a piece of glass, not backward, but normally. Then see it on the opposite side and reproduce it. But I do not believe our father did that. I feel certain his eye was so perfect, he was capable of just doing it backward and then reproducing it the same at other locations. Everyone knew his work was amazing.

But gilding was not all that he was able to paint. If you were old enough to remember the original outdoor advertising that was seen along highways and up on buildings, you knew it was not like it is today. Today large printed sheets of paper are affixed to the wooden boards that hold the advertisement. Sometimes today they are electronic signs. But, in the first half of the twentieth century these ads were painted by hand. There were cowboys riding their horses exclaiming how wonderful the cigarette was that they were holding in their fingers. Possibly there might be a person in the shower, with only shoulders exposed, praising the great bar of soap they were using. In other words, there were murals being painted on the billboards. They would be done by a special group of painters who could do more than just lettering. That comprised a much smaller groups of artisans. Their work was amazing. Our Dad accepted such jobs and had two people who could accomplish that work, Tony Schmidt and our father. There are numerous photos of them up on scaffolds doing their painting. But these were not like an artist who painted murals. Those non-commercial artists were not under time pressure to complete their work of art. But what Morris painted was not a work of art. They were advertising signs by companies that wanted their ads up rapidly. Morris and Tony would have to complete the entire painting in a matter of days or a week. The complexity of what the did in just a short period of time was astonishing. Painting a horse and a man with perfect facial features was all expected. They did it.

When I related the story about the outdoor gilding, I made reference to an effect of that which would later create problems for Morris. At some age, I cannot be certain, but possibly in his sixties, Morris suddenly stopped doing all the outdoor sign work and left it to Tony. The reason was that he suddenly developed a fear of being high up in the air on the scaffolds. Maybe on one of the assignments there were heavy winds that frightened him. Maybe on a job he slightly slipped and almost fell off. I cannot know what was the cause, but he just stopped doing that work and left it all to Tony.

No one was a more cherished employee than Tony Schmidt. When research began on this book, I knew it was necessary to find Tony. Many years had passed since they worked together. Morris had been retired for eleven years when he passed away. It took a great deal of searching to trace Tony down. He was considerably younger than our Dad. But he was no longer working. Unfortunately, at a very young age Tony had been afflicted with a stroke. When I met him again, he was in very poor medical condition. He was bedridden and having difficulty with breathing and swallowing. He had a very devoted wife who was taking great care of him. Because Tony and Morris were so close, his wife knew and spent time with Morris at the shop. They had one child who was still quite young when Morris and Tony were working together. In my interview with Tony he said, "My son was crazy about your father who was so attentive to him when I brought him to the shop. We took our son to a Japanese garden in the park near your house once when we visited with your Dad and Mom. The garden had little hills. From that point on he used to say the garden was called Morris' Mountain."

Tony did not want to stop talking about our Dad. Talking was not easy for him, and I repeatedly asked if we should end the interview so that he could rest. But he insisted on telling me more about our Dad. He was effusive in his praise about how talented our father was and "such a wonderful friend."

Much of what he told me was repetitive of what I had heard from so many others, like his constant happy spirit, his kindness and loyalty. But two items stood out from what I had known before. Tony told me they did so much work together in places where they would return to, every few years, for further working assignments. He said, "When we returned, I couldn't believe how he remembered the name of the building superintendent, the school principal or the priest from the Church. His memory was unbelievable."

The other thing that Tony kept bringing up was Morris' relationship to workers where he went. He told me you would not be able to determine the difference between the superintendent, the elevator operator and the cleaning people. He treated them all exactly the same way. Maybe that was because he knew what it meant to be either the lowest or the highest of the staff. He had been at all the levels himself.

I am not aware of any accidents that resulted from the work he did high in the air on scaffolds. But there were accidents.

Sometime, probably in the 1940's, the exact year has been difficult to trace, Morris took an assignment in Pottstown Pennsylvania. It must have been a very large job because it kept him there for weeks. On the weekends he would return home. It was there, certainly as a result of his deafness, he was struck by an automobile while crossing a street at night. He was hospitalized for some period of time due to injuries on his legs. My brother Arthur, who would later become an attorney, told me that lawyers had come to see our parents at home and cheated them into signing a document giving him a sum of money which was a pittance of what he deserved due to the accident. But our parents were so naïve as to the ways of the world that it was easy for those attorneys to take advantage of them.

This chapter on work would be incomplete without one further thought. Our father achieved great importance in his field. But it was by complete accident. It was not by his choosing, but rather the result of occurrences that directed his ultimate success. It certainly was an accident that when looking for work, he was hired by a painting contractor to be a paint mixer. It was not by any plan that the firm also employed a very fine painter named Alexander Larmour who had taken a liking to him. It was not by our father's choice that Larmour would become disenchanted with the firm and decide to quit and asked our father to quit as well and work for him.

It is not unusual for many people to have fallen into their life's work by circumstances not of their making. But since he was handicapped, it often made me wonder. With the level of intelligence he exhibited all through his childhood, were he not handicapped, where would his brilliance ultimately have led him? He did provide us with a clue.

Everyone who was exposed to him, fellow workers or clients who hired him, all agreed on one very humorous aspect of his personality. Each and every one of them could tell you about the strange quirk he possessed. Because of it everyone in his near vicinity as he worked, even if he was not visible behind a door or around a corner in the building, knew that Morris was there.

The quirk was the strange dissonant sound, not typical music, which they heard him humming. It was not soft and quiet. Everyone else could readily hear it. It was some strange kind of music he could hear in his brain. To him it was not dissonant. It would come from his throat constantly during his work. I'm certain he must have loved it.

It made me wonder whether music was deeply a part of his brain. If he were not deaf, might he have spent the entirety of is life is some aspect of music? Was he endowed with some wonderful musical ability that was thwarted by the act of nature that deprived him of the music the remainder of us hear?

For me the theory had an even more interesting turn of events. I spent a great deal of my life, even while I was creating a career in Medicine, trying to create a career in music. Since I had grown up in a world in which there was no music as a child at home, I never studied an instrument or had vocal training. As an adult, people would ask me how I became so interested in music with no exposure. I, of course, had no explanation. Then something changed my understanding.

When I married my spectacular wife Barbara, she had been a lifelong bridge player. There was nothing, absolutely nothing, she would ask of me to which I would not accede. So, when she asked very sweetly if I would agree to learn to play bridge and be her partner, I immediately studied the game. For years after that we played together.

Though I never cheated at the game, and was never rude to opposing players, I became the object of opponent's wrath on numerous occasions. They made it clear that they were not pleased. My faux pas occurred when I was confronted with a difficult choice of what card to play during a game. The opponent would turn to me and say, "Would you please stop that God-awful humming?" It would happen on a regular basis, apparently something I wasn't aware of. It made me think that the question of what directed me toward music, was a genetic pattern in my brain that led to music. It made me think that possibly it was something I had inherited from my father. Unconsciously, while contemplating a complicated decision I would revert to humming. I probably would never have achieved any great status in the world of music even with exposure during childhood. With our father's innate brilliance however, he would not be first handicapped child growing up in poverty to become a force in the world of music. But, we will never know.

Here Morris is at the top of the Philadelphia Museum of Art, made famous during the filming of Rocky. It must have been a very hot day because shockingly he is not wearing his usual suit jacket and tie.

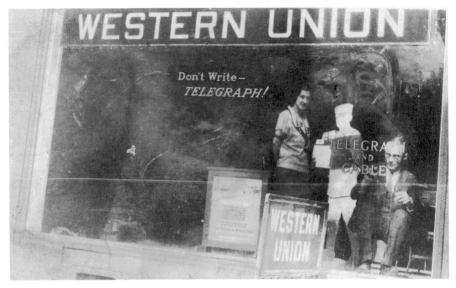

Here he is at work doing his reverse gilding on a Western Union window.

CHAPTER EIGHT
THE TRAIN WRECK

In mid January of 1963 the public transportation workers of Philadelphia went on strike. But Morris found a way to get to the center of the city. Through a plan, he made his way to the suburban Reading Railroad train station in Northeast Philadelphia. That train took him directly to the center of the city.

Everything was fine until Monday, January 21st. The weather was very cold that day but otherwise everything was fine until the train came to the terminal in center city where another train was stationery on the track at the station. The train on which he was a passenger plowed into the parked train. Passengers were hurtled around the cars. Two hundred and seventy-nine were hospitalized. Among them was our father. Fortunately, no one was killed. He was the oldest of the injured passengers at age 66, not surprisingly as it was early morning with workers headed to their jobs.

But, beside that, he was also the most seriously injured passenger. He was taken by ambulance to Hahnemann Hospital, where a half dozen years earlier I had graduated from Medical School. There he was found to have a fractured pelvis. But worse was yet to come. Within a short time, they discovered he had sustained a heart attack. Then in subsequent days he was identified as being diabetic. He had a long family history of diabetes. Since he rarely sought medical care, it is highly likely the diabetes pre-existed the train wreck.

He remained hospitalized for an extended period of time.

Nothing was ever the same after the accident. Of, course his injuries were severe and his recovery prolonged. But that was the least of the problems.

I do not know if the diagnosis was ever officially made by his doctors or on his charts, but there is no question he went into a state of significant depression after that. The light and happy spirit we all knew, which were an intrinsic part of his life was gone. It was for a good reason. Morris would never work again.

If there was one feature more than any other that described his life, it was the work that he did. Because of his ability and achievements, he had received considerable respect. The work provided him with great joy both while he was creating it and seeing it afterward. He flourished in the atmosphere of nothing being too difficult for him and no challenge he couldn't overcome. It suddenly ended and everything that was in the core of his very being was taken away. He would never recover from that loss. Nothing would demonstrate that more clearly than something which my brother, our cousin Bud and I were confronted with over the next few years.

Our father's talent was so special that the three of us all believed the best way for him to make a good recovery was to convert his talent into a new pastime which we were certain would bring back his spirit.

We began offering to supply materials for him to begin painting and drawing as an avocation. He could do it at home, chose his subjects and the results were bound to not only be wonderful, but raise his spirit as well.

For as many years as we tried, in whatever manner we attempted to get the process rolling, he absolutely refused. It would have been marvelous to have some lasting material thing to remember him by. By something was missing. His missed the relationship with fellow workers. He missed his role of running a very successful company. He must have missed the respect he achieved with so many important people, lawyers, accountants, business executives and on and on. We could not bring that back for him and he chose then to give up. No cajoling, love, or encouragement could overcome that depression.

Our father spent the remaining eleven years of his life almost exclusively with our mother, and the remainder of our family. He loved, as would be expected, to be with his many grandchildren. He never painted or drew another thing for the rest of his life.

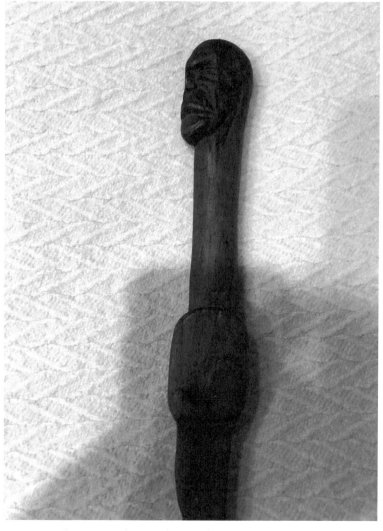

Above is a wood carving that is the single piece of his phenomenal carving talent that still remains.

This wood carving is the single piece of his phenomenal talent that still remains. No gilding of names on doors, probably numbering in the thousands, would still be present in the almost fifty years since his death. The gilding on the public buildings in Philadelphia are long since weathered away or demolished. The outdoor murals for advertising are no longer present anywhere.

He produced it sometime in his early adult life, possibly even before he met our mother. Then at a time which I cannot recall, he gave it as a present to me. In order that it not be forgotten, now that I am so old, I have passed it on to my son Chris. Hopefully, sometime in the future, he will pass it on to a descendant who has inherited Morris' artistic talent.

EPILOGUE

At the age of 78, in 1975, our father had a series of strokes and passed away. The last time I saw him in the hospital, though he had great difficulty communicating, he began crying as he said to me, "I'm not afraid of dying. I just hate to leave your mother." It was as great a love affair as one can possibly imagine.

After a long while our mother moved in with a man that both our parents knew in the deaf community. They lived together for a short while until our mother ended it. The thing I remember best about that time was a conversation my mother and I had after she ended that brief period of time with her deaf friend. She said to me, "Nobody was like your father!"

Morris Keyser was not a particularly large man, about 5 feet eight inches tall. He was slight of build though amazingly strong. He weighed probably about 140 pounds or so. But every ounce, and every inch could be found in just one organ of his body. Morris was 100% heart. He knew nothing of greed. He was totally selfless. It was as if some force had created a person that was the perfect combination of everything we would hope to find in an individual. Threaded through this heart of nothing but goodness and overwhelming kindness was a slice of brilliance. It allowed him, even with his handicap to run a business. He was totally unprepared. But he successfully accomplished that while assuming a leadership role. It allowed all who worked for him to have the greatest respect for his ability. Beyond that there was a gift of artistic proficiency that was difficult to surpass. The magical combination of all these traits was recognized by all who knew him. But, it was a time when the handicapped were thought so little of by the majority of the population.

It is not an exaggeration to state that he was the finest commercial artist in the entire area in which he worked from Washington, D.C. to New York. It was an opinion held by two experts who knew his work, Tony Schmidt and Morris' cousin Gerson. He had accomplished that status without the assistance of any training in art. He was exposed to the field by Alexander Larmour and then just from his own natural artistic talent became the special artist that everyone who worked for him or required his skills came to recognize.

Even though he did everything in the Larmour organization, he probably did not possess the skills to enlarge the company much beyond the confines of Philadelphia where the major businesses, charitable organizations and governmental organizations, schools, libraries, and museums all wanted him to provide the services they required.

At least one factor involved in the lack of expansion of Alexander Larmour and Company was Morris' total lack of any desire for fame, the absence of even a scintilla of materialism in his mindset and his complete inability to see himself as anyone special. He did not even ever consider himself handicapped.

On a personal basis, not one of us has the ability to select what will ultimately become our individual gene pool. It is all the luck of the draw. Within that package of genes we inherit, what may be included, are characteristics like meanness, cruelty, dishonesty, a lack of empathy and an assortment of personality features we might find distasteful. But one thing is certain. We have no choice in the matter. It is not possible for me to express the gratitude I feel to have been blessed with parents who brought to me a gene pool that provided me with the wonderful traits I saw in their lives. What I have done with that base they provided is a matter others will decide. But the opportunity it provided for me can never be repaid in full.

Because of all the things he accomplished, and all the goodness he innately possessed, I truly believe Morris Keyser, our father, was the unknown superstar.

ACKNOWLEDGMENTS

When one researches a book for more than forty years it is not hard to imagine they might forget some of the sources that made it possible to complete the project, especially when the author is approaching ninety two years of age.

I will be eternally grateful to all of those who helped me in my effort to accomplish a lifelong dream.

Among the most important were my mother, Diana Keyser, my brother, Arthur Keyser, my maternal grandparents, my aunt Pauline, resources at the Library of Congress, my father's cousin Simon, my father's most devoted employee, Tony Schmidt, my father's beloved teacher, Ms. Dalsemer, resources at the deaf school he attended, Bethlehem Steel and Lehigh University. The last three wanted to be helpful but could find no information that I could find useful.

Without the help of all these people I could never have assembled the story I so desperately wanted to tell. I thank them with all my heart.

If there are errors in the story I have told, I assume full responsibility for the mistakes. My intent was to accurately tell of the life of the most wonderful man I have ever known.

Herbert H. Keyser

Made in the USA
Columbia, SC
10 September 2024

41389424R00041